I Think I'll Start on Monday

I THINK I'LL START ON MONDAY

The Official 8½ oz. Mashed Potato Diet

by
TOTIE FIELDS

Illustrated by Cher Slater

A J. P. Tarcher, Inc. Book

**Hawthorn Books, Inc.
Publishers,
New York**

Totie Fields wishes to thank Arnie Kogen for his contribution to the text of this book.

I THINK I'LL START ON MONDAY

A J. P. Tarcher Book
Published by Hawthorn Books, Inc.

Designed by Jill Casty

3   4   5   6   7   8   9   10

DEDICATION

This book is dedicated to all those friends who at one time or another
tried to get me to go on a diet. . . . but failed miserably.

Moishe Budkofsky
Charlotte Weiss
Lenny Skeletsky
Ceil Levitt
Dody Krivitz
Tony Corrado
Mae Duddy
Jerry Bressler
Joanie Hammerman
Don Kileen
Paul Aboody
Gert Margolis
George Gilbert
Mr. Dominick
  (of Lookwell Barber)
Flowers by Cort
Lawrence Humphries
Elizabeth Courtney
Bob Mackie
Ray Agahyan
Bernie Silbert
Nan Freed
Lou Booth
Eddie Suez
Charlie Rapp

Joel Cassel
Jerome Alexander
Rose Altschur
Sue Kogen
Chickie Moskowitz
Sherry Hinderstein
Lillian Strachman
Ida Weiss
Harvey Shapiro
John Ferrari
Max Ackerman
Barbara Blatte
Norman Saval
Stan Richter
Leonard Solomon
Bob Stewart
Bob Simon
Jackie's (Vegas)
  Delicatessen
Shirley Freiberger
Sidney Kleinkopf
Stanley Navarre
Ray Weiss
Lil Skeletsky
Louie Levitt

Anita Corrado
Lyn Duddy
Bernie Hammerman
Abe Margolis
Harvey Silbert
Al Freed
Ferne Cassel
Jill Kogen
Howard Hinderstein
Lou Saval
Marty Lawrence
Barbara Dubinsky
Joe Sherriff
David Dushoff
Evelyn LaLonde
Sabena Feldman
Everett Finestone
Fran Shane
Louise Gerstein
Tracy Garfield
Hal Goldman
Jean Haden
Gladys Newman
Michael Lawrence
Henry Rubine

Bob Shad
Michael Mindich
Arlene Taub
Arnie Teich
Herb Zimmerman
Dave Youlovsky
Mae Feinstein
Ruddy the Omelette Man
Dick Curry
Blossom Horowitz
Chester Martell
Cantor Leibowitz
Edith Gormanzano
Sidney Leibowitz
Jay Kogen
Beverly Hinderstein
Linda Feldman
Al Feinstein
Chootch Penales
Jules Hoffman
Debbie Hinderstein
Eileen Sheriff
Doris Dushoff
Dallas Gerson
Howard Rothberg

Walter Holmes
Jim Daniels
Betty Ashley
Doris Sterling
Buddy LaLonde
Eli's Place for Steaks,
  Chicago
Bella Fishke
Larry Paskow
Harry Finley
Barry Feldman
Lorraine Finestone
Lola Paskin
Paul Ferrante
Ben Shane
Irving Gerstein
Viola Crump
Sylvia Sullivan
Murray Garfield
Rabbi Aaron Gold
Lou Bluestein
Father Bob
Abraham Hinderstein
Dr. Jeffrey Brown
Artie Dymn
Sam Sack
Ruth Marx
Joe Reich
David Lawrence
Le Etta Johnston

Harvey Ross
Herb Wolfe
Jim Rose
Warren Yablon
Herbert Fishbein
Dr. Ezra Greenspan
Dr. Morton Davidson
Netti Lawrence
Frank Shane
Herb Schwartz
Jo Ann Dale
Danny Stradella
Herb Wolk
Shirley Rhodes
Judy Tannen
Nat Dubinsky
Joe Mazzi
Betty Biddle
Joe Savino
Paul Winik
Barbara Goldman
Bill Haden
Kaye Hart
Louis Kaufman
John Bertera & Family
Marty Leshner
Adeline Murphy
Irving Newman
Howard Price
Sarah Rubine

Ann Mindich
Minnie Smith
Al Parker
Mann Scharf
Joe Taub
Joannie Teich
Gary's Wigs
Evelyn Zimmerman
Lillian Silbert
Sid Allen
Rose Youlovsky
Esther Lee Price
Sarah at Bloomingdale's
Margie Bryson
Albert Norotsky
Andre Correale
Marvin Block
Barry Brooks
Ashley Feinstein
Hymie Asnas
Bob Smith
Bob Jones
Marty Klein
Sid Zalkin
Manny Halbert
Lee Hinderstein
Dr. Sydney Reiff
Molly Shad
Edward Feldman
Jack Coughlin
Wendy Youlovsky

and especially to Georgie, Jody and Debbie

CONTENTS

HOW TO KNOW
WHEN IT'S TIME
TO GO ON A DIET 4

THIN MAY BE IN--
BUT FAT IS WHERE IT'S AT 6

WAYS TO LOOK THINNER
WITHOUT DIETING 8

FAT IS IN THE EYE
OF THE BEHOLDER 10

FIVE PRACTICAL
REASONS FOR NOT
GOING ON A DIET 12

ACCORDING TO MY WEIGHT
I SHOULD BE MUCH TALLER 14

THINGS THAT ARE
ROUND AND ARE
MUCH ADMIRED 16

SNAPPY
ANSWERS FOR
CHUBBY QUESTIONS 18

IT ALL BEGAN
WITH THE
RAW FRUIT DIET 22

FLAB
TECHNICIANS 23

LET THEM WATCH
THEIR OWN WEIGHT--
NOT MINE 25

CHUBBIES
ANONYMOUS 28

THE WATER DIET--
TRY IT, YOU'LL LEAK IT 29

CONFESSIONS OF A GIRL
WHO IS ON THE PILL 30

101 THINGS TO DO WITH COTTAGE CHEESE 32

MY FAVORITE ALL-TIME DIETS- THAT NEVER QUITE MADE IT 36

    1-The Bananas-Only Diet
    2-The Seven-Day Matzoh Ball-Beef Jerky Diet
    3-The Howard Johnson Diet
    4-The Onions Diet
    5-The Judge Crater Diet
    6-The Recycled Meatloaf Diet
    7-The Mexican Water Diet
    8-The 21-Day Knockwurst, Sauerkraut, Weinerschnitzel and Beer Diet
    9-The Sweet and Sour Cream Diet
    10-The Wizard of Oz Diet

TOTIE'S 2½ CALORIE A DAY DIET 41

TOTIE'S CALORIE CHART 42

HOW TO LOWER YOUR WEIGHT FROM 220 TO 219 44

THE SENSUOUS CHUBBY BY T. 46

SEX CALORIE CHART 48

FREAK OUT AT THE FAT FARM 50

DAILY ACTIVITY CALORIE LOSS CHART 54

JUST ONCE WON'T KILL ME 55

HOW COME YOU HAVE THAT FUNNY SMILE WHILE EATING CHOPPED TURNIPS? 60

NEW USES FOR OLD FAVORITES 62

ELEVEN THINGS
TO DO WITH
MELBA TOAST   64

HOW TO LET HIM
THINK YOU'RE ON A DIET-
EAT ONLY "QUIET" FOODS   65

TOTIE'S PHYSICAL
FITNESS PROGRAM   68

TRY THESE-
YOU'LL LIKE THEM   74

ONE THING
TO DO
WITH A CUCUMBER   75

DO-IT-YOURSELF
GYM ADVERTISEMENT   78

TOTIE'S
QUIZ SECTION   80

SO YOU THINK
YOU KNOW CALORIES   80

MATCH
THE CELEBRITY
TO HIS DIET   84

EAT IT-
IT'S GOOD FOR YOU   88

IDENTIFY EACH OF
THE FOLLOWING
SHAPES   90

MATCH
THE FOLLOWING
DELICIOUS FOODS
WITH THE DISEASE
THAT WILL OCCUR
IF YOU HAVE
TOO MUCH OF IT   92

TOTIE'S QUESTIONS
AND ANSWERS   96

A PRAYER
FOR CHUBBIES   98

DEFINITION: Diet—a system of starving yourself to death so you can live a little longer.

The first three letters in the word diet are "die," and at last count there were 23 million Americans who felt like doing just that, because they were on one.

Yes, 23 million Americans have gone diet crazy. Dieting has even replaced baseball as America's national pastime. In some cases our citizens combine activities. At a recent New York Mets-Pittsburgh game, the last three bottles thrown at the umpires were low calorie Fresca.

During the last few years we have been swamped with books, charts, lecturers, weight watching clubs, magazine articles—hundreds of sources of information about how to, where to, why to, what to and when to diet. But after all is said and done, there's really only one thing to know about diets. Which work and which don't. For instance, I once went on a crash diet for two weeks and all I lost was 14 days.

This book then is for all of you that are suffering through a diet or weight reduction plan. I sympathize with you. I know I had to go through the same thing when I was chubby, and if there is one thing I've learned from these terrible experiences, it is that it doesn't pay to "rush" into a diet. So sit back, relax, grab a Barracini with a cherry center and read my book. After all, you can always start on Monday.

3

HOW TO KNOW
WHEN IT'S TIME
TO GO ON A DIET

You may not believe this, but at one time I was very heavy. I realized it one year in Vegas when I was in a nude show chorus line. I was the last four girls on the end.

Before you even start to think about trying a diet, you must first determine whether you're overweight or not. There are often little telltale signs to indicate when you might consider going on a diet.

It's Time to Go on a Diet When

1. The man from Prudential offers you "Group Insurance."
2. You used to shop in the "Junior" department—now they send you to "Orthopedic Fashions."
3. You're standing on a corner in a red, white and blue outfit—and when you yawn strangers start to put letters in your mouth.

4. Ralph Nader insists you rotate your shoes every 4000 miles.

5. When you take a shower you have to "let out" the shower curtain.

6. When you are standing next to your car and get a ticket for double parking.

7. When friends start to photograph you with a wide-angle lens.

8. You wear all white to a party and the host shows movies on you.

9. You're standing on a bus and some men offer you their seats.

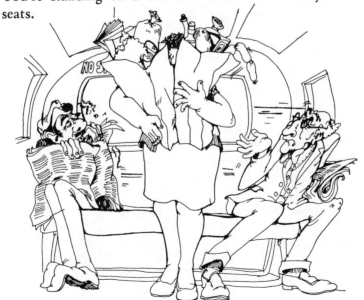

THIN MAY BE IN-
BUT FAT IS WHERE IT'S AT

In the past few years we've been conditioned into thinking thin is better than fat. We've been told the slim person is healthier, happier and gets to mingle with the Jet set. While the fatty is constantly fatigued, depressed and is seen hobnobbing socially at the roller derby.

Advertising, in particular, has been pushing thin over fat. You ever hear them touting "short, chubby" cigarettes? Of course not. No cigarette was ever called "Virginia Fats." Why didn't the lyrics read "short and stout and roly poly, the *Girl from Ipanima* goes waddling"? Could it be they're afraid to admit the real truth? That the chubby person is better off than the skinny.

6

If you don't believe me, just look at the U.S. Health Bureau of Statistics. They show that the fat person is less likely to:

1. Die of starvation in the Mojave Desert.
2. Give up quickly in an arm wrestling match.
3. Sink in Lake Erie.
4. Get whiplash on a Jack LaLanne Exercycle.

Besides, have you taken a good look at some of the thin people in history as compared to some of the chubbies? Take a gander at this partial list and see who you'd rather line up with.

Thin	Robust and Chubby
Scrooge	Santa Claus
The Iodine Skeleton	Aunt Jemima
Heinrich Himmler	Winston Churchill
Lucrezia Borgia	Sophia Loren

I think this should prove to you that thin people don't necessarily live longer, happier, more fulfilled lives.

WAYS TO LOOK THINNER WITHOUT DIETING

Looking thinner, not *being* thinner, is the real objective of many dieters and accounts for 98 percent of the girdle sales in America. But elastic can go just so far before it snaps. There are other methods of appearing thinner without the actual bother of tedious dieting which you might wish to consider.

1. Move to the rim of the Grand Canyon. Anyone looks thinner against a vast background.

2. Stand on your toes when you meet people.

3. Stay in your swimming pool up to your neck. People will think it's the waves giving your body that pudgy appearance.

4. Attend parties during a total eclipse.

5. Wear only solid colors.*

6. Eat nothing but garlic and limburger cheese. You won't lose weight, but you'll look thinner from a distance.

*If this doesn't work—wear stripes. I keep forgetting—I know it's either one or the other.

FAT IS IN THE EYE
OF THE BEHOLDER

How often have you heard the expression, "Fat is in the eye of the beholder"? Probably not too often because thin people control the television networks, major newspapers, leading magazines and a good portion of the matchbook cover advertising business, too. They have indoctrinated us into thinking a certain way. For instance, look at the two girls on the opposite page.

Obviously Girl A is as fat as Girl B—they just have their weight distributed differently. Everything is a matter of social and cultural upbringing. Oh, I guess, if you're judging by blue-collar, lower-middle-class tastes, Girl A might seem attractive (blue collar workers like her lower middle) but in the exotic, mysterious East, where they appreciate real beauty—in Burma, India, Ceylon, South Philadelphia—Girl B wins it hands down.

Yes, when Girl B takes off her girdle she has it all over Girl A.

Study the illustration. Look how clumsily Girl A's weight is distributed. She has such a nice face, too. It's a shame she had to let her figure go like that.

Girl A has unsightly curves, unevenly distributed, instead of having them lumped conveniently in one place like Girl B. Notice the unsightly bulges on Girl A—as opposed to the soft pleasant curves on Girl B. Girl A, obviously, has had silicone. Girl B also has had silicone. Unfortunately, it dropped. Observe A's spindly ankles—as opposed to firm, healthy ankles on Girl B.

Silicone

Soft
Pleasant
Curves

Unsightly
Bulges

Silicone
Dropped

Girl A

Girl B

Spindly
Ankles

Firm
Healthy
Ankles

FIVE PRACTICAL REASONS FOR NOT GOING ON A DIET

1. It's very impolite to leave food on your plate.

2. America is supposed to be the best fed nation in the world. Why make us look bad?

3. Fish, meat and vegetables may be chemically polluted. The U.S. Government has never found mercury in a chocolate layer cake.

4. Food is synonymous with love. If you diet, you're depriving yourself of much needed affection.

5. Sara Lee, Laura Scudder, Betty Crocker and "Mr. Hershey" are sincere, hard-working Americans. Check your conscience. Do you *really* want to take a living away from these people?

13

ACCORDING TO MY WEIGHT
I SHOULD BE MUCH TALLER

Weight is a relative thing. Now, my relatives think I'm too heavy. But then again, my relatives also think "spot reducing" is something they do at a dry cleaner's—and they think The Galloping Gourmet is a man who's drunk too much prune juice. But the less said about my relatives, the better.

You can go crazy trying to figure out what you should weigh. You know those charts that tell you height and weight? Well, according to that chart I'm not too heavy—I'm just too short! I found out that for my weight, I should be 12 feet, 4 inches tall.

If you're confused, on the next page is an Official Government Health Guide* as to what you actually should weigh:

*The Government of Nemtin, a border country between Bulgaria and Poland.

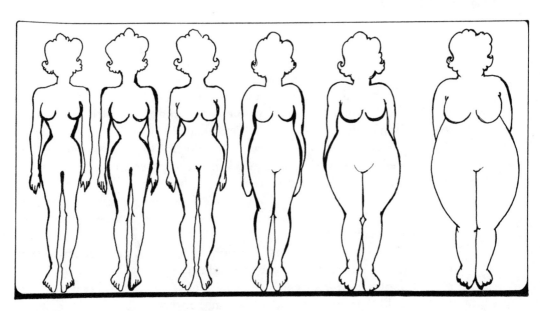

105 lbs.
"Emaciated"

115 lbs.
"Sickly"

130 lbs.
"Underfed"

152 lbs.
"Average"

170 lbs.
"Healthy"

194 lbs.
"Big boned"

THINGS THAT ARE ROUND AND ARE MUCH ADMIRED

Elizabeth
Taylor's ring

Don't you sometimes yearn for the good old days of Rubens and Raphael—when the chubby, the round and the "zoftic" were the female standards of beauty and excellence. (Who can ever forget Rubens' classic oil painting in 1632 of "Zoftic Girl With Water Jug"?)

Yes, those were the days when they appreciated size and substance. But that's all changed. Today we're living in the era of the "lose it," the "take it off," the "remove it." Everything's thinner, skinnier and smaller. Even our vocabulary. They've taken a lovely word like "Mrs." and made it "Ms."

Well, I just want to say that in spite of all the propaganda to the contrary it's no shame to be chubby and round today; because if you're rotund, look at the great company you're in. There are still many things in the world that are universally loved and also round:

Snoopy's nose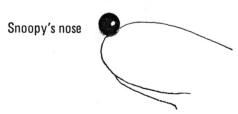

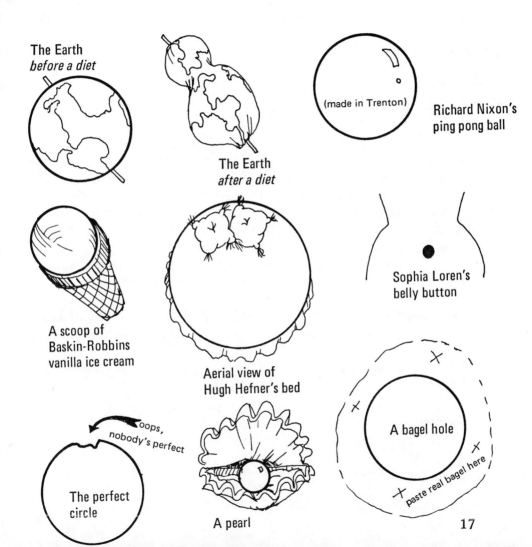

The Earth *before a diet*

The Earth *after a diet*

Richard Nixon's ping pong ball

(made in Trenton)

A scoop of Baskin-Robbins vanilla ice cream

Aerial view of Hugh Hefner's bed

Sophia Loren's belly button

oops, nobody's perfect

The perfect circle

A pearl

A bagel hole

paste real bagel here

17

SNAPPY ANSWERS FOR CHUBBY QUESTIONS

Overweight people are constantly barraged with insults. They have to put up with more ridicule than a Polish Edsel distributor. (God help him if he's a *chubby* Polish Edsel distributor.) Fatties bear the brunt of all physical humor and cruelty. You never hear anybody referred to as a "skinny slob." Comedians do gags about Mama Cass, Jackie Gleason and Kate Smith. When was the last time you heard a John Carradine joke?

I know how it feels because when I used to be heavy, I was also on the receiving end of many insults. Even well-meaning people would say, "I love to watch you laugh, Totie, 'cause so much of you has a good time." I'd smile outwardly at this cruel compliment. Then I'd rush home, lie down in my rooms and cry all night, letting the tears roll down my chins.

Yes. Fat people are constantly faced with insulting remarks and it's exhausting to think of comebacks. So I've done the work for you.

The following are some typical comments—and some suggested answers:

Q: Why are you fat?
A: I'm not fat. I just retain flesh.

Q: How did you get so fat?
A: I became pregnant and I never gave birth. My baby decided to live in.

Q: You have such a pretty face, how come you let your figure go?
A: Because—as hard as I tried, I couldn't let my "face go."

Q: Say, is that a spare tire you're getting around the stomach?
A: That's not my stomach—I'm just very low busted.

Q: Do you know it's not healthy to be too fat?
A: No. Hum a few bars.

Q: How did you get so fat?
A: When I was a kid I got the mumps and it never cleared up.

Q: Look at you. It's a crime to be so fat.
A: That's why I wear a girdle—to make the punishment fit the crime.

Q: How do you account for your chubbiness?
A: I have a bookkeeper.

Q: Why don't you tuck that napkin under your chins?
A: I will—after you sit down and put that chair under your brains.

Dieter's Memory Page

Heavenly coffee cake

Majestic chocolate souffle

21

IT ALL BEGAN
WITH THE
RAW FRUIT DIET

You may have gotten the impression that I hate to diet. That's not true. I love to diet. In fact, I'll diet on any kind of food I can get my hands on.

Many people think that dieting is a new fad. Actually, it's been with us since Adam. We all know that he was only allowed a half-cup of rhubarb—no apple!

It is not so well known, however, that one of the original Commandments was—Thou Shalt Not Covet Thy Neighbor's Eclair; since nobody knew what that was, it was eventually changed to "wife."

Even the Romans and Greeks were great dieters. All Julius Caesar ate was salad. In fact, he ate so many salads, they eventually named one after him. I think it's called the Julius Salad. And Socrates, with all his brilliance, never watched his diet. The poor guy died from drinking hemlock (712 calories per cup).

In the Dark Ages dieting was common. In those days it was called Starvation. This was followed years later by a fad that swept Europe—the Potato Famine Diet.

In the 16th Century, King Henry VIII inaugurated the "Quick Weight Loss Diet" with his wife—when he chopped off her head.

22

By the 18th Century, all of Europe was diet conscious. Marie Antoinette incensed the peasants and started a revolution when she shouted from the balcony at Versailles, "Let them eat Rye Krisp."

But that's all history. Today we've come a long way and there are thousands of diets to choose from. And it's hard to choose . . . because, truthfully, one is just as bad as another.

FLAB TECHNICIANS

A diet . . . that's doing without the food your doctor doesn't like.

That's right—it's his problem, not yours. The diet doctors are the ones who are causing all our suffering—putting our precious bodies through pain so that *they* can get satisfaction.

Most diet doctors don't even call themselves diet doctors. They call themselves "Internists." That's like a pickpocket giving himself the title "Self-Employed Fund Raiser," or a washroom attendant calling himself a "Director of Public Seating Arrangements."

These P.O.P.'s (Practioners of the Pudgy) always make promises. They say that within a month you'll lose 30—50—100—up to 150. Remember, what he's talking about is dollars, not pounds.

23

I'm proud to say that I've gotten some small measure of revenge. I have had only three diet doctors, and tragedy has followed all of them after each of my visits. Here is the sad tale.

The first dietician I ever had was Dr. Hans "Hands" Terwilliger. He went amuck after examining me for ten minutes—and was later found swinging from a chandelier at a Forest Hills chapter of Weight Watchers shouting, "You'll never take me alive."

The second one, a Dr. Edgar Firpo, attempted suicide by pounding himself senseless with a leafy vegetable. He was admitted to Mount Sinai Hospital with "roughage burns."

The final one was the most tragic. A Dr. Bernard ("Take the pill, it can't hurt you") Berman. After six months of treating me, he disappeared completely—and was discovered a beaten, broken man, years later in a Jersey City loft performing unnatural acts with cold cuts.

LET THEM WATCH THEIR OWN WEIGHT-- NOT MINE

Weight Watchers is a world-wide weight reducing club formed by Jean Nidetch. I can talk about Weight Watchers with affection—even though I was on their casualty list.

The thing I remember most about Weight Watchers was the weekly meetings. What a sight. I've never seen so many strange looking hippies—also strange looking thighsies, kneesies and tummies.

That's right. Every week 300 of the fattest people in the area would gather in one room and discuss their common problems—how to get out of the room.

It was crazy. It looked like the finals in the Miss Overactive Thyroid Contest.

The meeting was held on the ground floor—which was a good move. We had an unfortunate accident the week before when we all gathered on the roof of a condemned building.

What happens at these meetings? It's really exciting—members stand around and weigh their flounder.

That's what they do. All the members walk around with a little scale weighing their lunch. It didn't work for me. Everytime I put the spaghetti on the scale, it kept sliding off.

In addition to the little scale, there are other clues to identify a Weight Watcher. She is the one who walks into a dinner party with A) a blender, B) a packet of non-fat dry milk and C) a bowling bag. This is for carrying cantaloupe.

The Weight Watcher program also places a great emphasis on *fish*. They insist you eat fish at least five times a week. After four weeks on Weight Watchers, I looked great but I had a strange desire to spawn upstream. I sub-leased my apartment and lived in the belly of a whale.

When you're a Weight Watcher, your whole life is fish. I bought them. I ate them. I kept them as pets. You know how difficult it is to paper train a squid?

Not that you're limited to fish. No, they now have Weight Watcher Italian food, WW Chinese food and a WW Good Humor Special. You throw away the ice cream and eat the stick.

Weight Watchers are fanatics. One guy in our group had a bachelor party where the girl jumped naked out of a dietetic Danish!

All I can say is if you're unloved and chubby, after a year at Weight Watchers you're guaranteed to be popular. At $3 a visit, Jean Nidetch will love you! And if she doesn't, Chubbies Anonymous will!

CHUBBIES ANONYMOUS

Chubbies Anonymous is a fellowship of chubby men and women who have a common bond—we were all thrown out of Weight Watchers!

We join together each week to share our experiences, our strengths, our hopes and our Sara Lee pound cake.

We don't lose weight—but we do have fun.

Our biggest kick is calling dieters in the middle of the night, saying the word "pastrami" . . . and then quickly hanging up!

Another game we have is our version of Russian Roulette. We pass six glasses of skimmed milk around—and one of them is a vanilla malted.

THE WATER DIET--
TRY IT, YOU'LL LEAK IT

The Dr. Stillman Water Diet is a great diet. If you're a camel. Or a flounder (see Weight Watchers). Or Jacques Cousteau. For me, it's not too thrilling.

My husband, Georgie, and I went on the water diet together. My husband lost 10 pounds. I gained 70 gallons!

I drank eight glasses of water a day for a month. The water went all the way down to my feet. For four months I walked around with wet shoes. I even had to wear pumps.

Now, when you drink that much water it starts to affect you. Do you know that the first week of that diet, every night I had to sleep in Pampers? I think I'm the one that invented the water bed.

The inventor of the diet (Dr. Stillman) claimed that if you drink eight glasses of water a day and eat all the protein you can eat, you will lose 30 pounds in four weeks. I found out how he did it. His bladder fell out!

One thing Dr. Stillman did prove . . . you can lead a horse to water but you can't make her drink.

CONFESSIONS OF A GIRL
WHO IS ON THE PILL

Diet pills are the most effective of all reducing plans. You take them and within three weeks you can lose between 150—190 pounds— your husband! The side effects of pills make you so nervous and irritable that no human being can live with you.

Diet pills come in bright, lively colors. Remember 15 years ago when they said the "Reds" are going to destroy America? Now it's coming true.

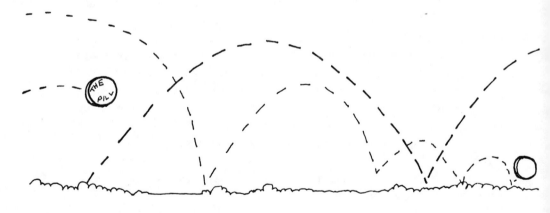

There are certain ways to recognize when you've been on diet pills too long.

1. When the sound of grass growing keeps you awake at night.
2. When you start to bite fingernails—*other* people's!
3. When you can't stand the sound of your eyelashes blinking.
4. When you think your vacuum cleaner is plotting against you.
5. When you start to heckle your minister.

101 THINGS TO DO
WITH COTTAGE CHEESE

Cottage cheese is the *one* ingredient that's listed on every single diet, and I don't know about you, but personally I'M SICK OF COTTAGE CHEESE!

Cottage cheese has been with us since Biblical times. The *real* story is that Lot's wife looked back and, instead of salt, was turned into a pillar of *low calorie cottage cheese* (large curd)!

In case you have any cottage cheese lying around the house, I've compiled this list of things you can do with it. You'll notice it includes everything but eating it.

1. Build a snowman.
2. Slip it in your teenager's bra. (You'll notice that suddenly she has more dates—and it's less expensive than silicone.)
3. Use it as a doorjamb
4. At night, rub it on your face instead of cold cream.
5. Throw it at a chubby bride.
6. Use it as a bookmark. (Not in this book.)
7. Line your sister-in-law's shelves with it.
8. Construct a life-size replica in the shape of Burt Reynolds.
9. Make a one-to-ten-thousand model of the Himalayas.

10. Put it on a leash and take it for a walk.

11. Color it green and sell it to the NFL as astroturf.

12. Build up the land dividers on the Pennsylvania Turnpike.

13. Mold it in the shape of a long rope. Then get two teams at each end and have a "Tug of Curd."

14. Light it up at a pot (cheese) party.

15.-101. Gift wrap it and give it to each of the 87 King Family members for their Christmas Special.

Dieter's Memory Page

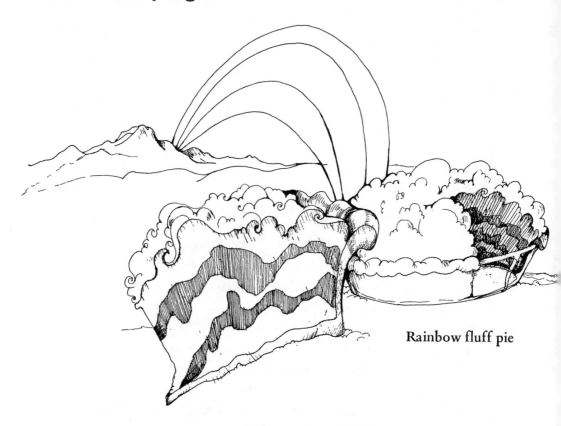

Rainbow fluff pie

Pancakes a la mode, plus

MY FAVORITE ALL-TIME DIETS- THAT NEVER QUITE MADE IT

1-The Bananas-Only Diet

Guaranteed for a rapid weight loss. Eat 16 bananas a day for a period of three weeks. You will quickly lose 20—25 pounds. Not from the diet, but as you swing from tree to tree to get away from your husband.

2 - The Seven-Day Matzoh Ball-Beef Jerky Diet

A must for chubby Jewish people living on the Kansas prairie. Also popular with rabbinical students who dropped out to become Marlboro men.

Take a medium-sized matzoh ball out of your pack, stick in a piece of beef jerky and let it bake in the prairie sun for seven days.

The weight loss comes as you lose your mind (4-6 pounds per mind) staring at this mess.

3 - The Howard Johnson Diet

You eat ice cream until your colon freezes! (Stay away from the fried clams—they're fattening.)

4 - The Onions Diet

Eat 18 onions a day. It makes you cry and you lose water.*

*You also lose friends!

5 - The Judge Crater Diet

Just follow this diet and one day you'll disappear completely.

6 - The Recycled Meatloaf Diet

For ecology fans. Eat nothing but recycled meatloaf for 42 days.

On the 43rd day a contingent from the Sierra Club will come to your gravesite.

7 - The Mexican Water Diet

You drink one glass of Mexican water a day. Somehow you manage to lose 15 pounds.

8 - The 21-Day Knockwurst, Sauerkraut, Weinerschnitzel and Beer Diet

I didn't want to put this diet in—I'm only following orders.

9 - The Sweet and Sour Cream Diet

This diet "confuses" the body into a dramatic weight loss.

Once the body is used to something sweet and then you suddenly hit it with something sour the body can't take it and goes all to pieces. This causes the calories to break down and at the same time bewilders the pituitary gland into a gigantic weight loss.

In this diet you are not confined to sweet cream and sour cream. There are other substitutes that also confuse the body:

1. Sweet and sour pork.

2. Sweet and sour pickles.

3. Hot and cold running water.

4. Slow and fast snails.

5. Early morning peas; late night parsnips.

6. Apple turnover; apple upstanding.

7. Hot cross buns; cold Star of David sponge cake.

39

10 - The Wizard of Oz Diet

Get dressed up as a witch and then have Liza Minnelli throw a pail of water on you. You will "melt" 20 pounds away.

TOTIE'S 2½ CALORIE A DAY DIET

BREAKFAST

3 bellybuttons from navel oranges
1 doughnut hole (unsugared)
5 scraped crumbs from burned toast
1 cup dehydrated coffee

LUNCH

3 plum pits
4 eyes from organic potato
1 guppy fin
1 glass tea steam

DINNER

1 chopped butterfly liver
2 lobster antennas
1 portion prime ribs of tadpole au jus
1 whiff of empty custard pie plate
1 cup of boiled out tablecloth stains

The above diet contains absolutely no calories. The 2½ calories are obtained when you tear out this page and chew the paper.

TOTIE'S
CALORIE CHART

Remember the good old days when people used to send you calendars? Now they send you calorie charts. This year I received one from my bank, one from a health spa and one from a funeral parlor with a cherry cheese pie attached.

I, for one, am sick of them. Everyone knows that a cup of beef broth is 75 calories, a cucumber is 10 calories and a chocolate bar with almonds is 295. And if you make a sandwich out of the above, with two slices of white bread, that's an additional 135. (Sounds crazy—but it's delicious!)

But these charts are not nearly thorough enough. They don't cover every single calorie we come into contact with in our everyday lives. There are dozens of things that put on weight when you're not looking.

If you want to remain healthy and trim, you have to watch *everything.* So, here then, is a list I've compiled. Cut it out and slip it in your wallet. It may come in handy.

CUT HERE ↗

Item	Calories
A dab of Crest	12
Breathing smog (per 24 hours)	8½
Licking your lips	2
Biting finger nails (per nail)	20
Swallowing finger nails	23
Watching The Doris Day Show	450
Watching The Doris Day Show (reruns)	225
Licking postage stamps	8
Biting the bottom of a cuddly, chubby baby	18
Driving through Hershey, Pa.	55
Dancing with Betty Crocker	360
Kissing Sara Lee	350
Checking into a motel with Laura Scudder	370

You can see that as surely as you live and breathe smog that an evening spent biting your nails as you babysit with your sister-in-law's chubby youngster (three baby bottom bites) in the back seat of a car, in a drive-in movie in Hershey, Pa., watching a Doris Day feature film (even more calories), followed by a dance with Betty Crocker and a late date with Laura Scudder, will add 1845 calories to your diet. So try to avoid this kind of evening.

HOW TO LOWER
YOUR WEIGHT
FROM 220 TO 219

The real trick to losing weight is not the diet or exercise—it's how you approach the scale. I ought to know. I've weighed myself so much, I have the letters D-E-T-E-C-T-O imprinted on the balls of my feet.

A scale is a delicate instrument and must be treated carefully. I'll never forget the first time I bought a brand new Detecto. I took it home and was about to step on it, when the scale looked up and pleaded, "Please be gentle; it's my first time."

Actually, the only important thing to remember when you step on a scale is that somehow you must weigh less than you did the last time you stepped on a scale. That's *all* that matters, and making sure that happens may require nothing more than improving your weighing technique.

Eleven Steps To a Lighter You:

1. Remove all clothing.

2. Trim finger and toe nails.

3. Shave legs, arms, head.

4. Clean wax from ears.

5. Brush teeth and use dental floss.

6. Remove lint from navel.

7. Sandpaper away all freckles.

8. Blot all perspiration.

9. Blow nose.

10. Empty mind.

11. Exhale!

Now . . . step on the scale. Good luck!

THE SENSUOUS CHUBBY
BY T.

Having sexual relations only burns up 120 calories, so it hardly seems worth it—but many of us like it anyway. What most people don't realize is that by carefully following a Sexual Activity Calorie Chart, they can love their way to thinness! Sex for dieters is an emotional substitute. When we can't get enough food, we have to "stuff ourselves with sex."

I like sex, but let's face it—it can't replace food. I get a sensuous thrill just biting into a muffin. I once ate a Ho-Ho to climax! I asked my husband Georgie for his brilliant thoughts about it. I said, "What's the strongest drive, sex or food?" He said, "Let's put it this way. I don't mind missing a meal now and then." Early in the marriage I said to Georgie, "You've got to make up your mind which room you want me to be great in—the kitchen or the bedroom. I can't be great in both rooms." He settled for the *kitchen*. With all my charms, I was surprised. I said, "Why?" He said, "Because I never heard of a pot roast getting a headache."

Recently our sex life has been fantastic. I've been on the "sex water diet." We have sex on a water bed *eight times a day* and when I don't want it, I claim I'm seasick!

All the recent best sellers have been about sex. "The Sensuous Woman" titillated us with such chapters as "The Butterfly Flick" and "The Whipped Cream Wriggle." Of course, we, on diet, are not allowed

whipped cream, but we
can create some erotic
lo-cal alternates such as:

> The Trembling Turnip
> The Red Snapper Romp
> The Pulsating Pot Cheese
> The Peeping Parsnip
>   (basic and advanced)

That's right. You can stick to
your diet *and* turn on your man with
these frenzied exercises:

1. Rub his body with Sego, and
   sprinkle with ¼ cup of finely
   chopped chives—then lo-cal
   your way to ecstasy.

2. Shut off all the lights (each watt is 14
   calories) and sit naked in a tub of
   Metrecal, while blotting yourself with
   Melba Toast.

3. Do a striptease in front of him—at the
   end wearing nothing but two poached eggs
   and a toast point over your strategic areas.

47

SEX
CALORIE CHART

Weight Loss During Sex

Sexual Activity	Calories Burned Up
Fumbling around	13
Kissing and petting	15
Foreplay	85
Three play	75
Shutting off Johnny Carson	4½
Having sex	110
Having sex with a Jewish wife	45
Having a headache during sex	28
Having an extra-marital affair	55
Petting to climax	135
Headache to climax	73
Having sex with 3 people	140
Having sex with 4 people	148
Having sex with 5 people	167
Having sex with 5 people and a water buffalo	183

Explaining to police about having sex
with 5 people and a water buffalo 12

49

Monday

Arrived at Fanny's Flab Farm and was greeted by instructor Hilda "the enforcer" Berkowitz. Weighed in, had a physical and then was told to get completely undressed—stand naked in front of a mirror—and "take stock of your assets and liabilities." I did. I'm <u>bankrupt</u> !!! Room assignments were made according to your individual needs. I was placed in intensive care.

Tuesday

Got up at 6 AM and had our usual breakfast—½ cup of black coffee (no cream, sugar, or <u>spoon</u>.) a poached egg and a tangerine pit. Exercised in 110 degree heat for 3 hours. It seems that I am attending Fort Dix for Women—and will be spending $800 to go on Bivouac.

Wednesday

Facial today. They used silly putty and meat tenderizer. and then I had my legs and thighs waxed. Sat for 15 minutes under sun lamp. Activities continued as usual through the <u>explosion</u> !

Thursday

Caused a disturbance in the dining room today when I asked for a scoop of ice cream on my melba toast. Cannot take this strict diet and exercise much longer. Cried myself to sleep tonight. Lost ¼ pound in tears.

Friday

Three of the other inmates and I "escaped" tonight. Snuck into town and had a pizza, ONION RINGs, COKE <u>AND</u> A CASE OF PETER PAUL ALMOND JOY.

Caught and dragged back to
camp by diabetic bloodhounds!

Saturday
Found behind the
dining room at 11 AM injecting
Sara Lee pound cake into
a major artery. Sent to the
"Punishment Room." Had
my mouth taped. Was fed ½
cup of rhubarb intravenously.

Sunday
CHECK OUT TIME!

Weighed in for the last time.
Gained 3½ pounds--
and for the first time in
my life measured 38-23-28
ON MY LEFT LEG!
Said Goodbye to all my
new friends--the owner,
the masseuse, the dietitian,
Hilda "the enforcer" and invited
them all to my house for
Coffee and Cake!

51

glasses of water a day!!

DIETER'S GRAFFITI

THERE IS NO Twiggy

Debbie Drake wears a girdle

Sidney Greenstreet is alive and well and living in the House Of Pies!

Mama Cass has a sweet tusk!

THE WORLD'S MOST EFFECTIVE WATER DIET!!

SOAP

WOMEN
FANNY'S
FLAB FARM

I can't believe I ate the Whole thing

Better well fed than DEAD!

DAILY ACTIVITY
CALORIE
LOSS CHART

No dieter can afford to ignore the daily hidden calorie input (see Totie's Calorie Chart), but attention must also be paid to the calories burned up during the stress and strain, the annoyance and frustration of our everyday lives.

Activity	Calories Burned Up
Suffering inwardly	19
Aggravation from a child	24
Aggravation from *your* child	240
Dialing a telephone	18
Dialing a princess telephone	16
Dialing a collect call	09
Having a hot flash	34½
Getting mugged	45
Mugging someone	49
Raising bail	$2500

Butting into a conversation 07
Changing your mind 3½
Changing someone else's mind 5700

JUST ONCE WON'T KILL ME

I'm one of the world's great dieters. I usually finish all the food on my four-week diet in only three days. Most authorities don't like this approach. They say that in order for you to stay slim, healthy and attractive you must stick to a diet and obey the rules. However, no doctor, no matter how strict, will insist that you stay on your diet *all the time.*

This is not possible. Everyone needs a break, and there are certain special occasions when it's perfectly all right to go off your diet. They are:

YOUR BIRTHDAY — A time for celebration. No one will deny you the right to do or eat whatever you want on *your* day.   1 day

HOLIDAYS — Christmas, Thanksgiving, George Washington's Birthday, New Year's, Fourth of July, Memorial Day—these are "feast days." It would be unhealthy (and un-American) to "do without" on these days.

12 days

RELIGIOUS HOLIDAYS — Easter, Passover, etc. These are sacred, religious occasions and we must not tamper with them. After all, who's more important—your diet doctor or God?

9 days

WHEN YOU'RE SICK — Your diet's important but your health comes first. If your doctor prescribes chicken noodle soup, ride pudding and buttermilk, who are we to argue?

18 days

WEEKENDS — A time for relaxing from the pressures of dieting during the rest of the week.

104 days

FRIDAYS — You can't just "jolt" yourself into a weekend of non-dieting; you must gradually get into it. Friday is the perfect day.

52 days

NBC WEEK — The new TV season. Only the "very strong willed" can be expected not to snack during this all-important week. 7 days

WHEN YOU'RE DEPRESSED — It is important for your "mental well being" that you munch on these days. 69 days

WINTERTIME — Summer, I can understand. Your body requires less food. But winter, your body needs energy *and* food. 91 days

ANN BLYTH'S BIRTHDAY — This lady donates her time to so many outstanding causes and has given us hours of joy on the screen. I think it only right that we feast in celebration. 1 day

This leaves only *one* day on the calendar for dieting. You can do it if you want, but it seems silly for only one day.

57

Dieter's Memory Page

Banana split boat

Chocolate layer cake

HOW COME YOU HAVE THAT FUNNY SMILE WHILE EATING CHOPPED TURNIPS?

No person in his right mind enjoys dieting itself; they just enjoy *talking* about it, and showing their friends that they can stick to it.

So, since the "appearance" of a diet is more important than the diet itself, here are some ways to convince your friends and spouse that you're on a diet—while at the same time reaping the benefits of healthy, scrumptious, high-calorie foods. All you need is a little ingenuity.

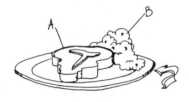

1. Chop orange sherbet and place it neatly on your plate next to your lean beef. It will look like chopped carrots.

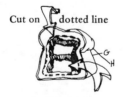

2. Cut open the inside of a loaf of whole wheat bread, leaving a large cavity. Then slip a Sara Lee pound cake inside.

3. "Poach" your ice cream. Then serve it over toast. It will look like the white of an egg.

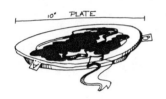

4. Instead of gravy, pour hot fudge over your roast beef. When your friends ask, "What's that?" tell them you like your gravy well done.

SCALE 1 - 1,000

5. A half a grapefruit is always impressive. No one need realize that as you're cutting and sectioning it, it is actually a miniature frozen "lime custard pie."

NEW USES FOR
OLD FAVORITES

All right, despite all my advice to the contrary, you've decided to go on a rigid diet and *stick to it*. You think that by staying away from French fried onion rings and Hershey's kisses you'll be able to attend that cocktail party in a size seven see-through dress instead of a giant Hefty bag.

Okay, if that's the way you want it, I'm not going to interfere. Stick to your diet. But don't suffer. That's right—even though you can't eat and swallow, there are *other* ways to get a thrill out of food.

Absolutely no diet doctor has ever said food can't touch "other" parts of your body. After all, why deprive yourself of the warm, sensual feeling you get just having food near your skin.

Here are some suggestions:

1. Sit on a marshmallow.
2. Run barefoot through a field of mashed potatoes.
3. Slowly back into a Tootsie Roll.

4. Relax in a tub of Whip and Chill.
5. Let M & M's melt in your hand.
6. Whip yourself with strands of linguine al dente.
7. Bring a veal cutlet over the state line for immoral purposes.

ELEVEN THINGS TO DO WITH MELBA TOAST

1. Take two and hang them from your ear lobes.
2. Place it under your mattress for more back support.
3. Use it as a finger splint.
4. Use them as lifts in a midget's shoes.
5. Paint it white and wear it as a pocket handkerchief.
6. Use them as shoulder pads.
7. Get 52 together and have a crummy card game.
8. Paste it on your lower abdomen and tell people it's an appendix scar.
9. Sell them to a medical center as tongue depressors.
10. Crumble one and feed it to obese sparrows.
11. Now that St. Christopher's demoted, mount a Melba toast on the dashboard of your car.

HOW TO LET HIM THINK YOU'RE ON A DIET— EAT ONLY "QUIET" FOODS

I weigh 127 in my shoes—163 *without* my shoes. My feet blow up when I take them off. My husband Georgie can't understand why I weigh as much as I do. The reason he is confused is because he never sees me eating.

Not only doesn't he *see* me eating; he also doesn't *hear* me eating. That's because I have mastered the art of eating only "quiet" foods.

That's right—the trick is to sneak off when he's in the other room and eat only "soft" foods so others won't hear you. Eat low calorie "loud" foods when you are with others, but great tasting "quiet" foods when they aren't looking.

It takes many years of experience to know what's quiet and what's noisy. Take Chinese food. Noodles are a no-no because they "crunch." Egg foo yong is great because it "slides" when it goes down. Some other "sliders" are linguini and Blue Point oysters. Lettuce is no good because it "crunches," cauliflower "crackles" and with asparagus you "gurgle." (It actually "slides" but you "gag" as you taste it, causing the gurgling.)

I've compiled a list for your convenience.

Quiet Foods

Butterscotch pudding

Baked Alaska

Ice cream (without sprinkles)

Pancake syrup

Cream of mushroom soup (if you don't slurp)

Meringue

Wedding cake (Only the main part. Not the little bride and groom standing on top. They make a terrible racket.)

Spaghetti (without meatballs)

Truffle (I don't know what this is, but it "sounds" soft.)

Noisy Foods

Mackerel

Carrots

Celery stalk

Melba toast (see *Eleven Things To Do With Melba Toast*)

Radishes

Low-Cal bubble gum

Can of salmon*

Rice Krispies

Swordfish (with sword still attached)

Diet cookies (much noisier than Mallomars)

It's not the salmon that's noisy. It's the can.

TOTIE'S PHYSICAL FITNESS PROGRAM

You had better undertake a physical fitness program because after going on a diet, you're going to be sick!

I'm a firm believer in the President's physical fitness program. President *Taft's* physical fitness program. (Our chunkiest President. His typical breakfast consisted of 3 glasses of juice, 22 eggs, 12 cups of coffee, and 38 miniature Danish with dietetic jelly.)

Aside from President Taft's program, I do only one exercise every day and it's worked wonders for me. Here it is:

Take your fingers and pat the fat under your chin for 20 minutes each day. Keep this up for six months. At the end of that time, notice how thin your fingers are.

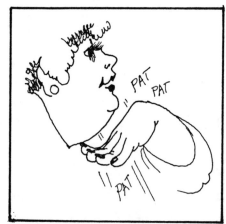

January 1, 1972

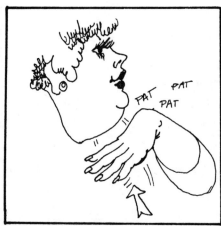

July 1, 1972

In recent years "military" exercise programs have been foisted on us.

I tried The Canadian Air Force Exercises for a year. What can I tell you? I ended up with a figure like a Mountie.

Then I tried The Swiss Navy Exercises. After a month of doing these daily, and getting better at it all the time, I discovered that there *is no* Swiss Navy and I stopped.

So I went to a diet doctor (see Flab Technicians, page 23) and he recommended I get involved in a sports program, but Joe Namath wasn't interested.

Leading physicians recommend the following sports as a healthy, invigorating way to help your figure:

BICYCLE RIDING — This seems like a nice, pleasant outdoor sport. But think about it. Do you want to be known as a girl who pedals it all over town? Of course not. There is a tremendous current revival of bicycling throughout the country. They say that it brings health and happiness. You know who this bicycle craze is making healthy and happy? The Schwinn Company.

If you must ride a bike there's only one way to do it—sitting on the handle bars while somebody else pedals.

I'll never forget riding on the handlebars in the bike scene of Butch Cassidy & The Sundance Kid. That's right; I auditioned for that scene with Paul Newman. It was so embarrassing. After two minutes they had to rotate the tires.

70

JOGGING — I tried jogging for three months. Everyone else loses weight. All I got was chafed!

SKIING — If you go skiing, not only won't you fail to lose weight, but you'll be guaranteed to *gain* six pounds. That's how much the average ankle cast weighs (six *and a half* pounds after the signatures are added).

For those who still want to burn off calories, there are some ways to do it on the ski slopes.

Activity	Calories Used Up
Wearing heavy thermal underwear	450
Spending a night with the ski instructor	665
Falling off the ski lift:	
Squaw Valley (elev. 8000 ft.)	580
Sugarbush (elev. 9000 ft.)	620
Aspen (elev. 12,000 ft.)	760

TENNIS — As a matter of principle, I will not participate in any sport that has a bat all chopped up like that.

WATER POLO — A lovely sport. I tried it once, but my horse kept sinking.

GOLF — Golf is too nerve-racking for me. The only time I played, I had to quit during the fifth hole. I kept hitting the little "windmill" as it was going around.

SWIMMING – I'd love to go swimming but I can't. The rule is you're not allowed to go swimming until two hours after you've stopped eating!

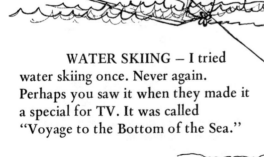

WATER SKIING – I tried water skiing once. Never again. Perhaps you saw it when they made it a special for TV. It was called "Voyage to the Bottom of the Sea."

TRY THESE-
YOU'LL LIKE THEM

There *are* however a few select sports I highly recommend participating in. The following contain all the exercise you'll ever need.

Floating

Dialing a maid

Turning on "Wide World of Sports"

Ping*

*Half of Ping-Pong. Just stand at one end of the table holding a racket in your hand. When you get proficient at this, you can then stand at the other end of the table and play the much more strenuous "Pong."

ONE THING
TO DO
WITH A CUCUMBER

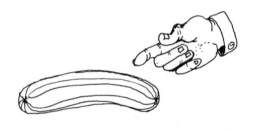

Dieter's Memory Page

Spaghetti supreme

Raspberry ice bombe

DO-IT-YOURSELF
GYM ADVERTISEMENT

Aren't you sick and tired of all those gym and figure salon ads that promise you quick, sensational results—and all you really lose is $11.50 a week? I know I am, and I'm sure many of you are too. Well, here's our chance to get even—and have fun besides. Simply fill in the numbered blanks from the corresponding numbered lists. You'll be able to construct your own gym, ad headline, and never have to go near one of those sweaty places.

I WENT TO (1) . . . .

WORLD RENOWNED (2) . . . . AND (3) . . . .

OFF (4) . . . .

OF (5) . . . . AFTER (6) . . . .

1

Jack LaLanne's
Debbie Drake's
Victor Bueno's
Burt Reynold's
Truman Capote's
The Godfather's
Howard Hughes'
Virginia Graham's
Portnoy's

2

Gym
Bathroom
Figure salon
Massage parlor
Motel room
Back seat of car
Water bed
Rumpus room
Closet filled with
warm tapioca

3

Took
Worked
Dwindled
Cursed
Shaved
Rolled
Sobbed
Exploded
Pummelled
Sizzled

4

30 pounds
6 pounds
½ pound
An inch
My underwear
My wig
3 layers
A whole bunch
A sliver

5

Ugly fat
Rather attractive fat
My behind
Freckles
Acne
Silicone
Dandruff
Glucose
My good arm

6

Only 4 days
2 weeks
11 years
Cardiac arrest
I backed into a pastrami slicer
My gall bladder operation
My menopause
A Timex torture test
A guy named Vito threatened
to beat me up

TOTIE'S QUIZ SECTION

Mainly because I'm not very good at them, I normally don't like tests. I once failed my aptitude test.

But, I think you'll like these. If nothing else, you'll at least lose 1/232nd of a pound turning each page.

SO YOU THINK YOU KNOW CALORIES

Multiple Choice Test

1. Which of these foods has the most calories?

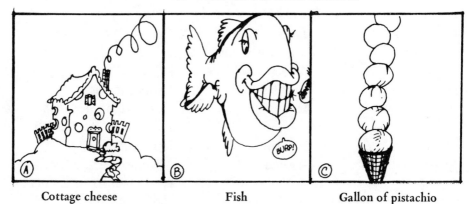

Cottage cheese   Fish   Gallon of pistachio ice cream

2. Which of these 21-year-old girls will live the longest?

3. Who is doing the best exercise?

Answers

QUESTION 1: (B) The *Fish* has the most calories. It happens to be a piranha, and just swallowed a 180-pound lady who was swimming in the river.

QUESTION 2: Girl C will live the longest. Girl A is Miss Honduras, and her chair is about to explode during a revolution in her country. Girl B is not a girl, but a female impersonator.

QUESTION 3: (B) Girls A and C are not exercising—they are "suffering." Girl B is exercising the "pursuit of happiness."

Spot The Mistake

See if you can spot the mistake in the following diet:

BREAKFAST

half-grapefruit

1 egg

1 slice white toast
   or portion of refined rice

dietetic jelly

tea or coffee

LUNCH

4 oz lean meat

moderate portion of rhubarb

1 sliced tomato

1 slice white bread with dietetic jelly

tea or coffee

DINNER

2 oz lean meat

moderate portion of carrots

roast suckling pig

moderate portion of refined rice

cooked fresh peaches

tea or coffee

SNACK

Plums, mid-afternoon or mid-evening

Answer

The mistake is obvious. There should be a period after the abbreviations for ounce.

MATCH
THE CELEBRITY
TO HIS DIET

This is one test that not only should be a lot of fun, but is also quite revealing. You can tell a lot about a person by the diet he is on. I remember once Ali McGraw and I were on the exact same diet—"The Lump of Farina & Raw Fruit Diet."

Of course, by looking at us now, you know the results—it worked beautifully for me, but Ali came out looking like a fat mess. I went over to her and said, "Lump means never having to say you're sorry!" As I left, she was punching me with raw fruit!

The idea of this test is to draw a line matching the celebrity to his diet.

After you finish, score ten points for every correct guess, and give yourself a smart smack on the knuckles for writing in my book.

A score of 30 or more indicates that you can probably prescribe for yourself; with 60–80 points you can make suggestions for others; and with 90 or more, you can become a lay diet doctor and really make some money. Then you can give up your diet entirely, because if you're rich, nobody cares if you're fat!

Celebrity	Diet
1. Virginia Graham	A. The Fruitcake Diet
2. Ernest Borgnine	B. The Mystery Diet
3. Howard Hughes	C. Fasting
4. Sabu	D. The Chicken Fat Diet
5. Dorothy Provine	E. The Petit Four Diet
6. The Galloping Gourmet	F. The Pancake Diet
7. Pat Boone	G. The Seven-Foot Hero Sandwich
8. Wilt Chamberlain	H. The White Bread & Apple Pie Diet
9. Mahatma Gandhi	I. The Pristine Diet
10. Aunt Jemima	J. Milk & Oreo Cookies
11. Eydie Gorme	K. The 8½ Oz. Mashed Potato Diet
12. Oscar Wilde	L. The "Elephant Salad" Diet

Dieter's Memory Page

All day Sunday soda

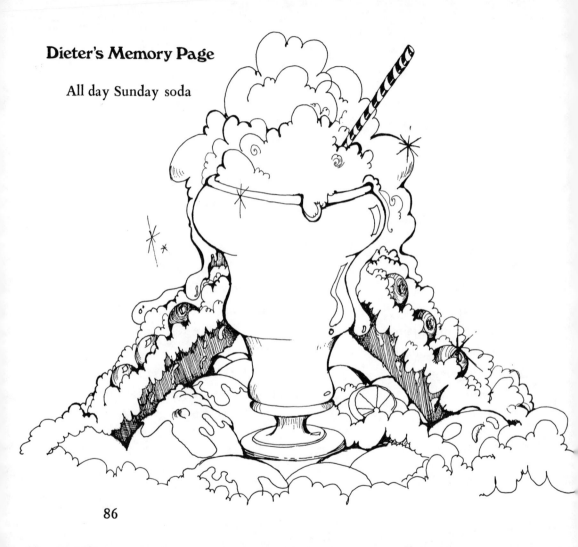

Circus delight

87

EAT IT-
IT'S GOOD FOR YOU

The following is material taken straight out of a best selling nutrition book. It tells you simply and clearly how vitamins, minerals and natural foods can make you feel better and look younger.

This certainly makes sense to me. So carefully read the following and then answer the questions below.

The amount of cholin required to maintain health is in proportion to the intake of solid, or saturated, fats in the diet; the more of such fats eaten, the more cholin needed. The exact requirement is not known but has been estimated to be between 3000 and 5000 milligrams per day. A serving of liver (¼ pound) supplies 500 to 700 milligrams; ½ cup of wheat germ, 400 milligrams; a heaping tablespoon of granular lecithin, 500 milligrams; an egg, 280 milligrams; a tablespoon of yeast, 40 to 180. Other foods are not rich. A serving of vegetables or meat may furnish only 10 to 50 milligrams of this vitamin.

Because cholin deficiency, by restricting the synthesis of lecithin, allows cholesterol to clog arteries throughout the body, it is vital that this vitamin be adequately supplied in the diet. A high blood cholesterol can be lowered by avoiding the solid, or saturated, fats (cocoanut oil, the fat of beef, pork and lamb, and all hydrogenated fats), thus decreasing the need for cholin; or by increasing the cholin content of the diet together with all nutrients necessary for lecithin formation. Fortunately both granular lecithin and vitamin supplements containing 1000 milligrams of cholin in a day's portion are available.

1. Can you have it with seltzer?
2. Would garlic bread be a good side dish?
3. If I restrict the synthesis of lecithin will I be able to get into a size seven dressy cotton?
4. How much does the above paragraph weigh?
5. What does the word "egg" mean?

IDENTIFY EACH OF
THE FOLLOWING SHAPES

1.

A. Extreme closeup of a calorie

B. Jello mold served to a bowler

C. A container of yogurt
    that has mildewed

2.

A. A Weight Watcher's pancreas

B. Dr. Stillman's key chain

C. A spaghetti on LSD

90

3.

A. A squashed blintz

B. A female corned beef sandwich

C. Bert Park's smile as seen
   by his tonsil

Answers

1. None of these. It is a pregnant crepe Suzette.
2. None of these. It is the Warsaw Freeway.
3. None of these. It's a dumpling's change of life.

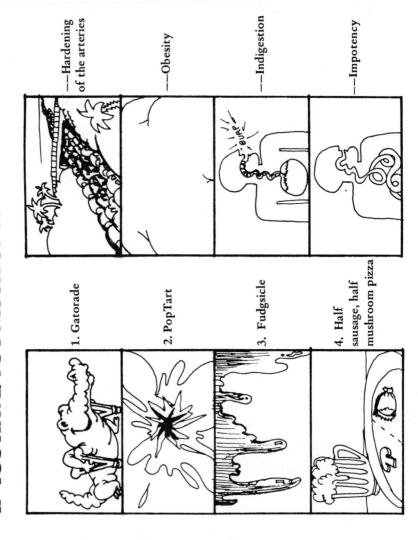

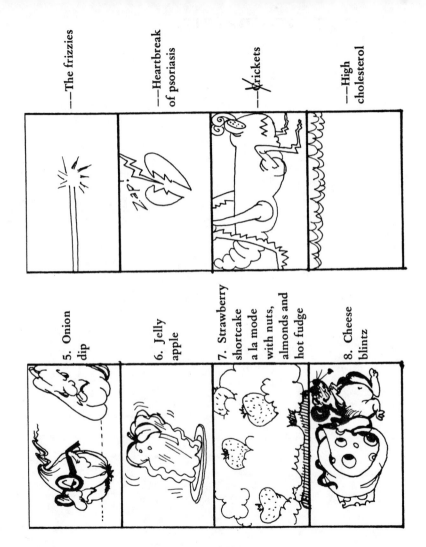

—The frizzies

—Heartbreak of psoriasis

—Crickets

—High cholesterol

5. Onion dip

6. Jelly apple

7. Strawberry shortcake a la mode with nuts, almonds and hot fudge

8. Cheese blintz

93

DIETER'S GRAFFITI

94

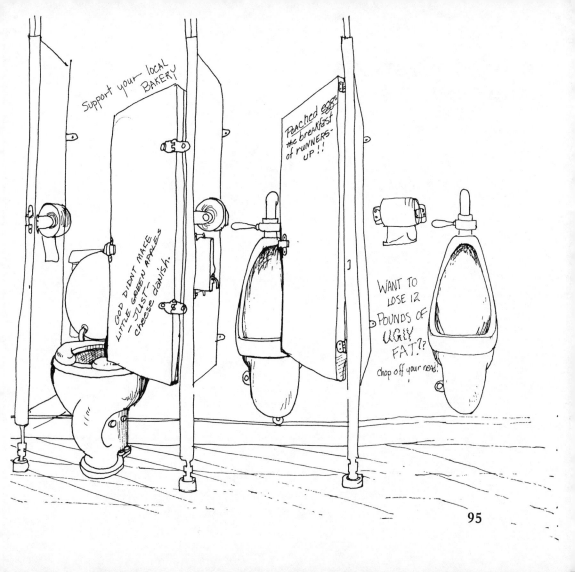

95

TOTIE'S QUESTIONS
AND ANSWERS

Dear Totie

Q: I weigh 240 pounds. What do you think I should give up?
A: Driving a Volkswagen.

Q: What do you think of the Metrecal diet?
A: I think Metrecal's great. I put it on everything—on my mashed potatoes, on peach Melba, on bread . . .

Q: I'm a bit overweight and I have a fashion problem. What do you think of hip huggers?

A: I think they're nasty little men.

Q: I'm on a special diet and suffer from acid indigestion. What should I do?

A: I have nothing but scorn for people who go on a special diet and suffer from acid indigestion. Who tells them to drink acid?

Q: Is there any pill that's guaranteed to keep my weight down?

A: Yes. A birth control pill. It will save you 11–20 pounds per pregnancy.

Q: Are there any glamor jobs for a young, attractive but "overweight" girl?

A: How about stewardess on a zeppelin?

Q: What kind of lingerie do you suggest for heavy women?

A I suggest a bra with three cups. You never can tell when you may have a blowout.

Q: You once said you had the same measurements as Ali McGraw. Is this true?

A: Yes. Her living room is 18 x 12 . . . and so is mine.

Q: Is chubbiness inherited?

A: That's a toughie. I could never answer that question . . . and neither could my mother, Kate Smith.

A PRAYER
FOR CHUBBIES

I look at life this way. I'd much rather be chubby and happy than thin and aggravated. And every night I get down on one knee (it's easier on the floor that way) and say a prayer of thanks that I don't have to go on one of those crazy diets. It goes like this:

My weight is my shepherd;
I shall not want lo-calorie foods.

It maketh me to munch on green guacamole;

It leadeth me beside the water bagels;

It restoreth my soul food;

It leadeth me in the paths of pastrami in delicatessens.

Yea, though I waddle through the valley of Weight Watchers,
I will fear no skim milk.

For my appetite is with me;

My Hostess "Twinkies" and "Ding Dongs" they comfort me;

They anointeth my body with calories;

My scale tippeth over!

Surely chubbiness and contentment shall follow me
all the days of my life.

And I shall dwell in the House of Pancakes—

Forever!